One Day in the
WOODS

One Day in the WOODS

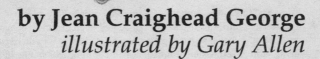

by Jean Craighead George
illustrated by Gary Allen

SCHOLASTIC INC.
New York Toronto London Auckland Sydney

ISBN 0-590-37944-5

Text copyright © 1988 by Jean Craighead George.
Illustrations copyright © 1988 by Gary Allen. All rights reserved.
Published by Scholastic Inc., 555 Broadway, New York, NY 10012,
by arrangement with HarperTrophy, a division of HarperCollins
Children's Books, a division of HarperCollins Publishers.
SCHOLASTIC and associated logos are trademarks and/or
registered trademarks of Scholastic Inc.

12 11 10 9 8 7 6 5 4 3 2   8 9/9 0 1 2 3/0

Printed in the U.S.A.   40

First Scholastic printing, October 1998

To Rebecca and Uncle Luke

One Day in the
WOODS

Chapter 1

A fat robin flew out of a beech tree at
5:52 A.M. It was the instant of sunrise on
May the third.

He *screak*ed. A young girl was
climbing his nest tree. His eggs were
under siege, his home threatened. His
cry alarmed his mate, and she sneaked
quietly off her nest but flew only as far
as a nearby twig. The girl was familiar.
She had climbed the nest tree before.

For the past several days Rebecca, a
ponytailed explorer, had explored the
robins' beech tree. She had climbed with

1

care, placing her feet firmly before she reached up through the yellow-green leaves of spring to take hold of the smooth gray limbs. Today she climbed more boldly and higher than she had ever gone before. Near the top she threw her leg over a strong limb and sat, feet dangling, one arm around the trunk. The robin returned to her nest.

Rebecca was in the canopy of the woods. The canopy is the top of five layers of plant life in the woodlands of the eastern United States. Under the canopy grows the shrub layer, a community of bushes, shrubs and young trees. Below the shrub layer is the field layer, where the ferns, wildflowers and ground cover of red partridgeberries and ground pine grow. Under the field layer lies the litter. This is a layer of fallen leaves and trees. It gathers tons of new material every autumn, and it would stack up to the treetops were it not for its residents, the fungi, bacteria and small animals. They convert the dead trees and leaves back to the soil from which they came. The soil is the bottom layer of the woods. Seeds and nuts take root there, find nourishment and grow into trees, shrubs and wildflowers.

Each layer is a neighborhood that shelters wild birds and beasts. Some never leave their friendly layers, eating, sleeping and raising young where they were born. Others wander through one or two layers; and still others, like the squirrels, make use of every neighborhood—from the canopy, where they collect nuts, to the soil, where they bury them.

Rebecca looked down through the

layers that together make up the glorious community called the Northeastern Deciduous Forest, the forest of falling leaves. Poets call it the woods.

The tree sitter was not thinking about the five layers of the woods this spring day; she was in the beech tree to find an ovenbird, a warbler whose home is the deep woodland. "When you find an ovenbird," her uncle Luke, a naturalist, had said, "you will have found the wizard of the woods."

Finding a wizard was Rebecca's idea of a worthwhile expedition. She had gotten up before dawn, packed a lunch and walked down the dim trail into Teatown Woods, a beautiful woodland in the Hudson Highlands of New York.

She began climbing the beech tree at sunrise.

"I'll know an ovenbird," she said to herself. "Uncle Luke said it's a wizard. A wizard does magic. That's easy." Rebecca settled herself in the tree crotch as comfortably as she could.

"Uncle Luke also said the ovenbird has large eyes that sparkle like a woodland lake. Its white breast is streaked with black tear-shaped jewels, and it wears an orange cap on its head. It sings, 'Teacher, teacher,' with a voice so loud it can drown out a brass band. Then he said something strange: You don't have to find the ovenbird; the ovenbird will find you if you sit very still. I am sitting very still and no ovenbird has found me."

What Uncle Luke had not told Rebecca was which layer or neighborhood the ovenbird lived in, and so she was searching the rustling canopy, where warblers fly.

Chapter 2

A gray screech owl, who had stopped his hunting at sunrise, soared to the beech tree and quietly slipped into his hollow. He hunted by night and slept by day. Rebecca grew uncomfortable. She shifted her position, and her magnifying glass slid out of her daypack. It fell, knocking against the yellow male flowers of the beech tree and exploding their pollen into the air. The pollen touched down on clusters of pale female flowers and had them fertilized by the

time the magnifying glass hit the ground.

Rebecca always carried this glass when she walked in Teatown Woods, a reservation near her home set aside by her neighbors to preserve a beautiful bit of primeval woodland. Uncle Luke had given her the magnifying glass for her birthday. He had showed her how it made small things more enchanting. It magnified tiny flowers into large bells, and insects into perky monsters. Small fish became whales at sea. Little dewdrops looked like big puddles under the lens of the magnifying glass.

She heard it hit the ground, looked down and saw it propped against a twig. She would get it when she climbed down.

As the sun rose higher, it shone through the transparent new spring leaves of the many kinds of trees in the woods. Each glowed with a different shade of green.

The beeches shone yellow-green, the sugar maple leaflets were a pale

pinkish-green, the chestnut oaks were olive-green and the ash trees gleamed silver-green. There were blue-greens, orange-greens, gray-greens. The spring woods on May the third were a cathedral window of more than one hundred fifty sunlit greens, a different color for each species of tree. By June all the differences would be gone, and the forested landscape would be solid June-green.

Into the beech tree sailed a small black-tan-and-silver squirrel, a flying squirrel. She coasted like a paper airplane through the twigs and alighted on a branch not far from Rebecca. Upon seeing her, the squirrel did an amazing thing: She walked boldly down a thin twig to within inches of Rebecca's face. The flying squirrel was not afraid of human beings, for she had never seen one before. She lived in the canopy, where no people lived, and she went about her duties at night, when most people were asleep.

At 7:15 A.M. on May the third, Rebecca held out her hand. The sleek squirrel sniffed, then stepped upon it.

"Now, this," said Rebecca, "is wizardry to me."

"Good morning," she added softly. The flying squirrel studied her with large eyes that were as black as space. When her curiosity was satisfied, she gathered all four of her tiny paws under her and jumped. Furry skin unfolded like sails between her front and back feet, and she soared downward. Alighting on a tree trunk, she ran a few steps, then popped into her nest hole.

She curled over her kits, who had been born the night before under the waning spring moon.

"A squirrel who flies and sits on my hand," said Rebecca. "How much more wonderful can the ovenbird be?"

A raccoon, who had heard Rebecca's voice, was looking up at her from a den in a large hollow near the bottom of the beech tree. It was spring, and she, like the flying squirrel and many other mammals in the woodland neighborhoods, had babies to tend. She *chuttered* her annoyance at being disturbed. Her cubs whimpered for food, and she dropped out of sight to nurse them.

The canopy was quiet at 8 o'clock. Rebecca listened, looked and waited.

A red-eyed vireo flew into the woods and alighted on a twig near Rebecca. The bird had just arrived from Brazil after a month's long flight. Like the flying squirrel, the vireo lived in the canopy; but unlike the flying squirrel, he

almost never went out of his neighborhood. He found his food and met his mate there, and they built their nest up in the small branches and twigs of the canopy.

Other birds of the treetop neighborhood were awake. A flock of golden-crowned kinglets flitted past Rebecca on their way north. Some brightly colored warblers who feasted on the millions of tiny insects in the canopy winged by. A downy woodpecker drilled into the tree trunk for a beetle larva.

The sun rose higher. Leaf-mining wasps landed on the tender leaves and began to lay eggs. A butterfly of the canopy flitted around a tree flower.

Near Rebecca's nose, a tiny gypsy moth caterpillar spun out a long thread of silk. A breeze caught it and carried it up in the air. The larva held on to it and went sailing out over the woods like a balloonist. It would travel to a woods less crowded with its own kind. There it would settle down, eat tree leaves and

grow to be an inch and a half long before spinning a cocoon.

Rebecca saw many things by sitting still, but no ovenbird came to the sunny neighborhood at the top of the trees.

Chapter 3

She decided to look for him in another neighborhood. Climbing down, she passed through the dark shrub layer of mountain laurel, viburnum and young beech and maple trees. A cardinal lived here all year around. He was a permanent resident of the shrub layer.

The air grew slightly warmer as Rebecca neared the ground. The climate of the woods varies from season to season and layer to layer, but not very much. Unlike the desert and the alpine tundra, the woodland is a moderate spot.

The trees temper its climate. In summer their leaves cast shadows that cool the ground and air. In the leafless wintertime and in early spring when the leaves are small, the sun shines down and warms the ground and air as it was doing when Rebecca dropped out of the beech. All year the tree trunks and limbs slow down the winds and change them into breezes. In spring and summer the tree leaves break sheets of rain into large drops that fall upon the shrubs. The shrubs break the drops into droplets that splash gently down on the wild-flowers and ferns below. The splashes trickle earthward on wildflower stems and seep quietly into the litter. In winter the fallen leaves hold the snow, and when it melts, they catch the melt in their curled cups. The cups decay and ease the water into the soil without eroding it. In this manner the trees moderate the climate of the woods. The woods are not too hot or too cold, too wet or too dry. They are a gentle place.

For these reasons, and because the deciduous woods, meaning the woods of the falling leaves, grow in the northern temperate zone of the Earth, foresters call them "the temperate forest." On the average, rainfall ranges between 40 and 50 inches a year, and the temperature ranges between 0 and 90 degrees Fahrenheit.

This lovely forest lies in the eastern United States as far north as southern Maine and as far south as the foothills of the Appalachian Mountains of Tennessee. Called wildwood in Great Britain, the deciduous forest once covered England and temperate Europe, fading out in western USSR. In Asia it grows in the eastern middle of China, in Korea and in Japan. Many of the same families of trees grow in this great forest the world around; beeches, maples, oaks, ashes, birches and their neighbors. Their presence supports the theory that there was once but one continent on the Earth, Pangaea. When that ancient continent pulled apart and drifted, the trees were carried to new and widely separated homes. Over the eons they changed slightly in their new environments, but not much. Today the woods of America look very much like the woods of England, Europe and Asia. Many of the same wildflowers grow in the field layers the world around.

Wherever they are, the woods are loved by people. They have laced them with footpaths and trails that lead around waterfalls and lakes, up mountains, along ridges, under vaulting trees and over rocks. People walk in the woods to watch birds and mammals, to admire the wildflowers and to sit and wonder at the wild freshness of the forest of the falling leaves.

On May the third in North America, the Teatown Woods were hiding a wizard, and Rebecca was determined to find him. She dropped onto the soft forest litter and tiptoed into the flowers of the field layer. White bloodroots and

20

mayapples were blooming. Pink spring beauties and a few yellow dog-toothed violets were opening their petals. On the third of May the woods flowers were racing to bloom before the tree leaves came fully out and cut off their sunlight. Rebecca burrowed down among the flowers and sat so still that the keen-eyed Cooper's hawk, who was hunting small birds and mammals, did not even see her as he flew through the canopy.

The sun rose higher. Its rays angled more steeply.

Before noon they shone down through the magnifying glass. It concentrated them into a hot brilliant star on the forest litter.

A thin twist of smoke arose.

Chapter 4

Rebecca listened for the loud voice of the ovenbird. The leaves rustled. A bird appeared. It was not an ovenbird but a chestnut-sided towhee. He scratched in the forest litter and kicked up leaves as he looked for food. The towhee visited several neighborhoods. He hunted in the forest litter, nested in the shrubs and sang his song from the bottom of the canopy. His song, like all the music of the songbirds, had several meanings. This morning he was saying to other males of his kind, "Keep off my property."

Tomorrow this same song would be sung to his mate, but the meaning would change. He would be saying to her he had land, food and nesting sites—a bird's wealth. If his property pleased her, she would settle down and raise a family with him.

A chipmunk popped out of the doorway of a labyrinth she had dug through the litter deep into the soil. She ran in Rebecca's direction, nimbly dodging a cluster of yellow wood violets.

The Cooper's hawk returned. With a

chirp of fright the chipmunk dived into the greenery. The night-loving wood rat crouched on his belly to make himself inconspicuous, and a hungry shrew stopped foraging and ducked under a leaf.

The Cooper's hawk flew on by. The chipmunk came out from under the ferns, saw no hawk and ran home. The wood rat slunk to his nest, but the shrew stayed out in spite of the hungry hawk. The shrew was reckless. She had an enormous appetite and had to eat both night and day. She kicked up the leaves looking for food, letting the sunlight into the dark underworld of the litter. The light disturbed the residents. Tiny mites, sowbugs and spiders scrambled for cover. Millipedes rippled away on their many feet. A beautiful wood snail slid slowly over a wiry white fungus and hid under a leaf. An earthworm that had come to the surface to eat the dead leaves and, unknowingly, convert them into soil, squeezed his muscles and shot

down out of sight. Slugs and centipedes winced at the light and burrowed deeper. The litter layer is a crowded neighborhood. Rebecca got down on her hands and knees to look at the small residents—and remembered her magnifying glass.

She ran back to the beech tree and stopped still—horrified. Her magnifying glass had started a fire that might destroy the reservation. Before she could get her jacket off to smother it, the flames flared up. They quickly burned the driest leaves on the top of the litter, and as quickly died down. Rebecca threw her coat on the dying flames.

Now the five layers of the woods worked their wizardry. At 11 A.M. a strong wind that would have fanned the fire higher struck the edge of the Teatown Woods. It was slowed to a breeze by the trees. The breeze was slowed to a breath by the shrubs and wildflowers, the breath became a stillness under the beech tree. In the stillness the fire burned

downward. It reached the puddles of winter snowmelt and spring rain held captive in the dead leaves. It sizzled and went out.

Chapter 5

Rebecca pulled back the litter to make certain no sparks smoldered under the surface. She saw none. Anxious to make sure the fire was out, she emptied her jar of lemonade on the burn, ran to the woodland pond and scooped up water. At the pond's edge she knelt under graceful hemlock trees with lacy needles and pagodalike limbs. They are one of the specialized plants that make vertical communities in the woods.

Just as there are layers, so are there vertical neighborhoods in the deciduous

forest. Around the streams and ponds
live the water-loving plants and animals,
hemlocks, liverworts and frogs. When
old trees fall to the earth, they leave
holes in the canopy and the sunlight
pours in. The sun lovers are able to
grow: saplings, bushes and shrubs. They
make up the neighborhood of the woodland copse. On the rocky ridges where
the soil is thin, pine trees take root, twist
toward the sun and shelter porcupines
and bracken ferns. This is the ridge
community. Where fires or farmers have
cleared large tracts of trees, grasses and
field flowers take hold and create the

woodland meadow. In the lowlands where the rain and snow melt settle in the spring, the mire-happy plants appear: red maples, royal ferns, sphagnum moss and sedges. This is the woodland swamp.

There is one more vertical neighborhood in the woods, the most peaceful and haunting of them all. It is the woodland park. The trees are old and so healthy that their dense leaves cut off the sunlight. Nothing grows on the floor of the woodland park, not even ferns. Very few animals live there, for fear of being exposed to enemies in the openness. The shadows are blue-green, the litter very deep. Silence is a presence there.

Not far from Rebecca, who was kneeling at the pond's edge, stood a woodland park. If she had looked over her shoulder, she would have seen it.

But she did not. She was concentrating on filling her jar. A female wood duck appeared in the middle of the pond. For a moment Rebecca thought a wand had been waved, so instantly did the duck materialize. She wondered if this was some of the oven-bird's wizardry and remained still.

The female wood duck lifted the crest of feathers on her head. This was the bird's signal meaning "come." The male materialized at the call. His red eyes were circled with white and iridescent-green feathers. His cheeks and breast were purple, his wing coverts black and white, his plumes red-violet.

"You are gorgeous," Rebecca said under her breath. The female did not look at her stunning mate. Her eyes were on a pileated woodpecker's old nest hole in an ash tree. She called. Her

voice was so low, Rebecca thought she was hearing the wind blowing through thistledown.

Inside the hollow a newly hatched duckling heard clearly. He jumped up two feet, fell back, jumped up again and dug the sharp hooks on the ends of his toes into the woody wall. He jabbed another hook at the end of his beak into the tree wood and climbed like a fly four feet up to the nest entrance. The hooks themselves are a bit of wizardry. They have evolved over the eons to enable the flightless ducklings to climb out of their deep nests. When the little birds reach the doorway, the hooks begin to disappear immediately. Having served their one purpose, they are no longer needed.

The walnut-sized duckling looked down forty feet to the ground. He jumped. Fluttering and pumping his feet, he hit the ground with a thump, gained his balance and ran into the water. Eleven downy gold-and-brown brothers and sisters followed him.

33

Rebecca watched in amazement as one by one they fell a distance that would have killed any other babies. Unhurt, they ran like windup toys to the pond.

Although Rebecca was standing perfectly still, her eyes blinked; and that was enough movement to catch the father wood duck's attention. He saw her. By lifting his feathers he told his perky little brood to follow him. They swam toward the drooping hemlock boughs. The mother flapped her wings dramatically; and Rebecca did exactly what the wood duck wanted her to do: She glanced away from the ducklings to look at her. When she glanced back, the ducklings were gone, leaving no clues for an enemy.

"The wood ducks are wizards, too," she said. "What can the ovenbird do that is more magical than falling forty feet and playing tricks on my eyes?"

Chapter 6

She carried her water-filled jar along the shortest route to the beech tree, a straight line through the copse. It was a neighborhood of viburnum bushes, young maples and hickory saplings and the shiny-leafed mountain laurel. The towhee lived there. A doe jumped to her feet and snorted. Her fawn stood up. Before Rebecca could say "Oh," mother and fawn were bounding on their long swift legs. As they sped, they lifted their tails to show the white underfur, a warning to other deer to hide. Near the

35

pond they stopped. Their tails went down. With that, they vanished. Although Rebecca was staring right at them, she could not see the white-tailed deer. When they stood still, their colors blended into the trees and bushes and were diffused by the lights and shadows. Rebecca could not see the deer for the woods.

"Deer wizardry," she concluded. "It seems to me, dear Uncle Luke, that there are a lot of wizards in the woods, not just one."

Rebecca reached the burn, dumped the water and sat down to eat her lunch where she could keep her eye on the dead fire. She also tied her magnifying glass to her daypack to make sure that accident would not happen again.

The odor of smoke had disturbed a skunk. He was shifting around in his leaf-filled hollow in a log trying to avoid the terrible smell. He gave up. At 2 P.M. he left his den and walked slowly in front of Rebecca, not three feet away. She held her nose and sat very still. The skunk's tail was arched, his head level with the ground. He did not even bother to see if Rebecca was dangerous. His weapon of acrid, eye-burning musk, which he could shoot almost twenty feet, rendered him fearless. The skunk walked slowly. His confidence was superb.

"You are another wizard," Rebecca said when the skunk had ambled into the copse. "And I really cannot say which one of you is the best."

Chapter 7

It was after two o'clock and she had not seen the ovenbird. Satisfied that the fire was out, she wandered down the trail, looking from right to left. At the pond she glanced over her shoulder and noticed the woodland park.

"I've looked everywhere but there," she said. "Although there is no place for a bird to hide there, I might as well look." Into the woodland park she strode.

The canopy arched high above her. The tall tree trunks rose clean and straight toward the sun. The park floor was open and quiet, the shadows silky. She tiptoed to a rock and sat down.

"If I believed in gnomes," she said to herself, "I would say this was their home." Wide-eyed, she looked around.

A brown-gold leaf on a dead twig on the ground twisted slowly, then fluttered and disappeared.

"What was that?"

"Teacher, teacher."

Rebecca looked up the slope.

"The ovenbird!" she exclaimed. "It's in the copse." She stole up the slope into the sapling grove and frightened the male towhee resting there.

"Teacher! teacher! teacher!" Now the call was coming from the woodland pond. Rebecca trod quietly to its brink. She saw the wood ducks dabbling for food and a tiny frog—but no ovenbird.

"Teacher! teacher! teacher! teacher! teacher! teacher!" The sound was as loud as a trumpet blare.

"He's in the woodland swamp." She

tramped down to the lowlands where the red maples grew.

At 3 P.M. Rebecca was still looking for the ovenbird. She had found an opossum, two frogs and the footprints of a gray fox in the woodland swamp, but no ovenbird.

He sang from the ridge. She climbed up the rocks. In the cozy pine community she discovered a porcupine sleeping in a tree crotch, but no ovenbird. He called from the woodland park. She ran back. He was not there.

"I give up," she said, sitting down on the rock. "You sing from everywhere. Is

that your wizardry? That's not so great. The deer vanished before my eyes. The wood ducks fell forty feet. The squirrel flew like a bird, and the skunk was not afraid of me." She thought a moment. "Even a voiceless little caterpillar went ballooning. What's so great about singing from many different places?"

Rebecca put her chin in her hands and stared at the woodland floor.

"Teacher! teacher! teacher!"

"I hear you in the swamp again," she said, staring at the brown-gold leaf again. A large black eye looked at her. A bird with orange hood and black-streaked breast took shape. She grinned.

"There you are. Now I know why Uncle Luke called you a wizard. You're a ventriloquist. You have been singing from that same twig all afternoon."

The ovenbird had returned from Mexico two days before but had not sung. Instead, he had sneaked silently around his old homestead, checking on the food supply, locating his enemies and noting the abundance of materials for his nest. There was an ample supply of dry fallen leaves with which to build a dome over his rootlet-lined nest. This dome, which looks like an old-fashioned clay oven, is the reason for his name, ovenbird.

He and his mate were members of the woodland park community and lived close to the ground, as do all ovenbirds. They build their nests in the litter, cover them with leaves and raise their young there. The males, to protect themselves from enemies, who could easily hear and then see them in the openness of the

43

woodland parks, can throw their voices like ventriloquists.

"I have seen a lot of wizards today," Rebecca said to the bird without speaking out loud. "Being a ventriloquist is very clever, but the flying squirrel sat on my hand, the wood ducklings fell forty feet, the deer vanished before my eyes. What makes you so special?"

The ovenbird spread his wings and flew. He took a straight course through the understory to the canopy and the sky. High above Rebecca he hovered on fluttering wings.

And burst into song. This song was a flute warble, a clarinet trill, a tumbling, rising serenade of love. It was an aria of rapture, a song to announce good nesting sites, abundant food, deep, rich litter, a cool, dark woodland park, rootlets for nest-making, dry leaves for domes. He sang long about these things. At 6 P.M. he stopped his serenade and fluttered on his wings.

The day was almost over. The sun was near the edge of the earth. It was time for Rebecca to go home. She adjusted her daypack.

In the rosy twilight the ovenbird folded his wings to his body and fell. On his plummet to earth, he spiraled and twisted and looped. He cavorted and danced. And he sang. He sounded like flutes and trumpets, clarinets and wood pipes. He filled the air with incredible sounds.

He plunged through the canopy, past the new leaves and tree flowers, down into the shadowy park. He alighted at Rebecca's feet and looked up at her.

"You *are* the wizard of the woods," she said. "You are." The bird cocked an eye at Rebecca, and she stared fondly at him. Each saw something different.

The ovenbird saw that Rebecca was not his mate.

Rebecca saw a wizard.

Before the sun set on May the third, all was well with the woods. Rebecca had seen the wizard. The flying squirrel was soaring. The raccoon was nursing. The deer were grazing. The ducklings were under their mother's wings and the caterpillar was ballooning eastward on the prevailing winds.

And that, at 7:54 P.M. when the sun went down, was the wizardry of the woods.

Bibliography

Brockman, C. Frank. *Trees of North America.* New York: Golden Press, 1968.

Dudley, Ruth H. *Our American Trees.* New York: Crowell, 1956.

Durrell, Gerald. *A Practical Guide for the Amateur Naturalist.* New York: Alfred A. Knopf, 1983.

Farb, Peter. *The Forest.* New York: Time-Life Books, 1969.

Farrand, John F. Jr., ed. *The Audubon Society Master Guide to Birding,* Vol. 3, *Old-World Warblers to Sparrows.* Garden City, N.Y.: Alfred A. Knopf, 1983.

Ketchum, Richard M. *The Secret Life of the Forest.* New York: American Heritage, 1970.

Kohl, Judith and Herbert. *The View from the Oak.* San Francisco/New York: Sierra Club Books/Charles Scribner's Sons, 1977.

Little, Elbert L. *The Audubon Society Field Guide to North American Trees.* New York: Alfred A. Knopf, 1980.

Naden, Corinne J. *Woodlands Around the World.* New York: Watts, 1973.

Peterson, Roger Tory and Margaret McKenny. *A Field Guide to the Wildflowers of Northeastern and North Central North America.* Boston: Houghton Mifflin Company, 1968.

Selsam, Millicent. *Maple Tree.* New York: Morrow, 1968.

Index

Page numbers in *italics* refer to illustrations.

51

A naturalist and animal lover, **JEAN CRAIGHEAD GEORGE** has taken in one hundred and seventy-three pets over the years, including raccoons, skunks, robins, iguanas, and wood ducks. "Most of these wild animals depart in autumn when the sun changes their behavior and they feel the urge to migrate or go off alone. But while they are with me, they become characters in my stories." Jean Craighead George is the author of many nature books for children, including the Newbery Medal–winning JULIE OF THE WOLVES and its sequel, JULIE. She lives in Chappaqua, New York.

"I began drawing before I could talk," says **GARY ALLEN**. "My family always knew I would become an artist, because I constantly drew pictures on the wall as high as I could reach." Gary Allen went on to study art at the State University of New York College at New Paltz and is now a designer at The Culinary Institute of America in Hyde Park, New York. He lives in High Falls, New York, with his wife and stepson.